Surviving The End Times

DERRICK WHITSY JR

Copyright 2017

FB : End Times Survivors

<u>Disclaimer</u>

Table of Contents

End – Times Survival Guide

This End Times Survival Guide is for those of you that are **serious** about what is happening in the world **today**. You **MUST** understand that MAJOR things are happening **right now** in the world that is going to change our lives **FOREVER**! It is for those of you that are willing to make the necessary decisions for both you and your loved ones. These are the times which **require** us to be vigilant and unified like never before. God has already told us that we wrestle not against flesh and blood but against **spiritual wickedness in high places**.

And it is these individuals, pawns on the earth, whom seek to destroy us from the face of the earth. This is the type of truth that many people cannot swallow. It interrupts their "5 Year" plans and disrupts their "leisure" time. You **will not find the truth on TV**, for it is controlled by a few individuals that control the entire world. This is so that you will not know what their True agenda is. But there are many Alternative Media outlets that share the unbridled truth with us. It is time for you (if you aren't already) to wake up for it is past time for the people of the world to see what we have unfolding before us.

Billions of people are going to perish in these coming times, but the bigger picture is that there is an afterlife, therefore you must know where you would spend eternity if you died tonight.

It is imperative that you understand the magnitude of this and the importance with it.

Life as we know it is changing forever and YOU must be prepared for these things!*

This Guide is going to detail 4 main areas which you need to be informed about and aware of.

    A.)Salvation
    B.)Current World Affairs
    C.)Preparation Details
    D.)Opportunities

Each section is a critical area in which we all need to be in tune with as a people. I can guarantee that you also will come up with a number of ideas of your own that will be of benefit to you and your family. This guide serves as a basic layout of what to be aware of.

****

Salvation

Before we can get into the physical preparation behind this; the foundation of it all must be set. Much of this won't make a lot of sense or matter much to you if the spiritual preparation of the equation isn't addressed.

- You must understand that Spiritual Warfare is, and has been happening, since the fall of mankind. The Enemy (Spiritual Wickedness In High Places), seeks to destroy you, I, and at least 7 Billion other people on the planet. This same number, is also outlined in the Bible, therefore this indicates that God is using using/allowing these entities to play their role in His purpose for the world.

- The thing that **YOU** must know is, if you died **tonight**, where would you spend eternity? For it is in these desperate times that you must absolutely know what the Truth is. You simply cannot afford to just "go along" with the flow anymore. Your Eternal soul is at stake! And War is upon us; you are a soldier rather you want to be or not!

- We are all about to be tested greater than we ever have before in the history of human existence! Therefore you **MUST** know that if you died tonight, would **YOU** be counted worthy to inherit the Kingdom Of God?

- Are you Saved? Do you Know Jesus Christ as your Lord And Savior? He died on the cross for you and I, and wants you in His Kingdom when you leave this Earth. Here's how you receive Salvation :

1.) **Repent Of your Sins** : Make a conscious decision in your **heart and mind** to turn away from your sins, and live your life according to God's Holy Word, His Commandments. God has a standard for us; there is a certain "Way" that we are supposed to live our Lives. We cannot just live life as we please, doing as we want.

2.) **Believe in your Heart, and confess with your mouth, that Jesus Christ is the Son Of God :** You must know that there is only one way to Heaven. Yes, there are multiple beliefs out here in the world, but the fact of the matter is that it is literally impossible for everyone to be "right" about what they "believe" in. Humbly ask God to reveal Himself to you and lead you to the truth. Jesus died so that we could have the opportunity to be in Heaven when we leave this earth. He will forgive you of all your sins, cleanse you of all your iniquities, and save you from Eternal Hellfire.

3.) **Endure And Obey God's Word :** It Is not enough to just "Believe" in Jesus, demons believe in Jesus also, and tremble. We must Obey His commandments and endure the trials and tribulations of life with out falling away. We must be ready and watching day and night for His Return. We must constantly be praying, fasting, and reading God's Word so that we may receive power from Him to be able to stand against the attacks of the enemy.

God isn't commanding us to be robots, but He has established a definite order and Holy Lifestyle for us to live by. It is by **His** Standards that we are measured and not our own. There is **100% Freedom in Living your Life for God**. Freedom from the Chains and Bondages and Vices of Life that keep people in entangled in a web which they have no hope of escaping without Jesus.

And It is In **THESE TIMES** that **YOUR** Faith will be **DIRECTLY** tested by extremely evil forces of people that seek your demise.

<u>Chapter 1</u>

<u>Current World Affairs</u>

There are a number of things happening **<u>right now</u>** in the world but this Guide will only touch on the major areas that you need to be informed about and aware of. You **<u>MUST</u>** discuss this information/these topics with your loved ones. Everyone in your family absolutely needs to be in the know about these things, so that you all can be on the same page and within the same prepared state of mind. No one has to be an "expert" or "know it all" when it comes to this stuff, just someone who has a basic understanding of **<u>Reality</u>**. You cannot afford to be around someone that is going to get you captured, injured, or killed. They are a severe liability to you and everything you love.

A.)<u>Economy</u> : From just a snap shot of what is happening at this moment, and what has been happening for some time now, you will see that the countries of the world are falling apart one by one. America (which is the daughter of Rome, the modern day Babylon), is falling apart right before our eyes. The US Dollar, a Fiat Currency Ponzi Scheme, Which has been in place for over a century, is collapsing at this moment. This year, 2016, marks a Jubilee year, which is the 50th Year coming right after a 49 year cycle (7 years = Schmita), and it has shown throughout history to be the year that a catastrophic event transpires. Examples of Schmita years.

- 2022 : We can only imagine what is going to happen during this/next year. Based on what has taken place during the years of 2020 and 2021; we can clearly all see the great shift that has taken place in the wake of the Covid Pandemic. Many businesses around the world were forced to close their doors due to the epdemic.

- 2015 : Market Closed, Lost Over 1000 points In A Day, China Devalued Currency, Lost 2 Trillion Dollars, etc. Its HAPPENING!

- 2008 (7 years) : Stock Market Collapse. Housing Market

- 2001 (7 Years) : Stock Market Collapse. Internet Bubble

- 1994 (7 years) : Stock Market Collapse. Spanish Crisis

- 1987 (7 years) : Stock Market Collapse. Black Monday.

Social order will fall to pieces as this nation is handed over into Anarchy and Chaos followed shortly by Martial Law. People will be desperate to survive as they simply will not be able to **<u>afford</u>** to live their lifestyle. Most people will lose their homes and be forced to live in the streets. This is the **<u>definite</u>** path that America is headed down. It is **<u>Judgment from God</u>** for the disobedience of this nation and its Idolatry. This "country/federal corporation" is currently becoming a 3rd world nation. Many people are going to perish during this time as looting/robbery, murder, and all types of evil immorality engulfs every state.

As of the most recent events, this year of 2020, we have seen and felt a number of things unfold all around us and within our lives. This book was originally written and published in 2016, so obviously, many things have transpired over the past four + years. From Trump being elected, to the Coronavirus, to Economic lockdowns and Pandemic lockdowns, bombings, mass wildfires in Australia, etc. There has also been mass protests happening all over the world, and the exposing of mass human trafficking and pedophilia amongst the Elite rulers of the World.

This year of 2020 has been the year of exposure like never before seen. So many more people have been awakening to the Truths of this World and how it all really works. It is a serious time for us all and should be a sign to us all that we need to press back in to God and take our walk with Him more serious. Most of the laws that need to be passed to transform our world into a Nightmare have already been passed. Bill Gates holds the Patent on the technology that will be used to program the RFID Chip/ Mark of the Beast. You can find the information on that Technology under "Publication W0/2020/060606"; notice the 666 pattern in the Publication numbering itself. The Book of Revelations, as discussed later on, tells us the numerical value of the Mark of the Beast system.

The (experimental) Vaccine Is being pushed on the masses right now at this point for a Virus that has a 99% survival rate. I strongly suggest against taking the Vaccine just based on common sense logic alone. Why would you take a Vaccine that was released in record time and that has not been fully tested? Why put your body through that type of risk? This is the same Government that experimented on black people in the 1900s when they purposely injected them with Syphilis. Why would anyone trust anything they say when it comes to this type of information? Below are a few of the things we have to look forward to coming soon.

B.) **FEMA Camps** : There are right now at this moment in time, several hundred FEMA Camps AKA Modern day holocaust camps, all over America, including here in Tennessee. Once the economy collapses and social order falls apart, people all over this country will be rounded up and taken these "holding" centers. You do not want to be taken to one of these as there will be no returning once you are there. You will not be able to be with your spouse as you will be separated as soon as you arrive. These places are **ALREADY** fully staffed and open, ready to go.

C.) **World War III** : This War is currently unfolding before us, as you can see at this moment, a number of nations have invaded Syria under the "guise" of going after "ISIS". ISIS is a false flag terrorist group that is meant to play a role in drawing the nations into World War III. It will by far be the most bloody war in human history. There will be no distinguishing between soldier and civilian. America, Europe and other Allies against Russia, China, Cuba, Iran, and other nations. I will not sugar coat things with you all so I will just be straight up and tell you that America Will Lose this war.

- This has nothing, **Zilch**, to do with being "Anti-American". It is **100% Biblical Prophecy** and it is already coming to pass right before our very eyes. America is **Already** a defeated nation.
- America will be invaded from the south, west and east coast. It will also be taken down from the inside. The Russian and Chinese Armies are much stronger than the US Army and as we are told in Book of Daniel and Revelations, this country will be overcome.
- Martial Law will be fully established all over the America once the system collapses, and since America's collapse will bring about the entire fall the global economy, Martial Law will established Globally Under the New World Order agenda. There will be a curfew. There will be numerous more violent "incidents" between police and civilians, armed militias, etc.
- Whenever a nation lives in disobedience to God, He hands them over into the hands of a foreign enemy. All throughout the Old Testament in the Bible, we see God handing the Children of Israel over into hands their enemy when they lived in Disobedience to God. And here we have again, America, which has lived contrary to God's laws for a very long time now.
- Nuclear Warfare will be a major catalyst in this war that extinguishes much of the human life on this planet. Practically all of the major cities will be nuked and wiped from the map entirely. We can clearly see in the news how America and North Korea have been verbally threatening each other with Nuclear Warfare.

D.) Natural Disasters : These natural disasters serve as severe tools of Judgment against America. They have already been striking all over the world but for here in America, the target states are New York, California, and Florida, which are considered by God to be Sodom and Gomorrah. It is those places that will be wiped out by both Natural Disasters and enemy Invasion. Earthquakes and Tsunamis will tear America apart and many people will perish during these perilous times. In 2017, we have seen natural disasters ravaging America; Florida and Texas were hit by Hurricane and massive flooding. California and most of the Western part of the US has been on fire constantly, and Puerto Rico was also hit by a major Hurricane.

E.) <u>Biblical Prophecy</u> : If you look at what is happening right now in the world, humble yourself, and ask God to lead you to the truth, you will see that we are indeed at the very end of time. Biblical Prophecy is unfolding right before our eyes as each nation falls deeper into sinful depravity.

- **<u>The Great Tribulation</u> :** This period of human history will begin very shortly once the Antichrist comes to power. He is already in Office right now and is only waiting on the right time to reveal himself. There are currently FEMA Camps all over America, INCLUDING here in this city and all over the state. **<u>People will be taken from their homes and taken to these "holding" camps</u>. <u>You do not want to be captured during these roundups! You do not want to end up one of these "camps"!</u>** There will be <u>**LAWLESSNESS**</u> during this time. You must be hidden in God and TRULY abiding in Him!

- **<u>New World Order</u>** : For centuries now there have been world leaders who have gone and <u>**PUBLIC RECORD**</u>, and openly promoted this very evil agenda, which also is spoken about in the Bible. Even America's very own presidents have openly spoken about such things. There is agenda depopulation of the human species down to 500 Million people. **<u>That is over 7 billion people exterminated from the face of the earth</u>**. This "agenda" of "theirs" is SPELLED out in the Bible, and aligns up perfectly. What chances do you think that you have at surviving this? I am going to be straight up and tell you that those chances are extremely slim, and for those that are alive, they will have the Mark Of The Beast, whilst everyone else will have to live in captivity, ie, the mountains, caves, bunkers, etc.

This will be even worse for you if you are a Christian, for we will be hunted down like wild animals, just as they are being hunted down <u>**RIGHT NOW**</u> in various Middle Eastern locations. The Antichrist, whom will be in power very soon, by my calculations, less than a year from now, is going to declare Christianity to be illegal and we are going to viewed as terrorists. Even the civilian population will be completely against us. The people will not be able to think for their selves as they will be programmed via the RFID chip to only follow orders and do exactly as the new "World Leader" (Lucifer) says. Christians whom are captured will have to die for their faith In Jesus, and will persecuted globally. Our Faith will be tested like never before. Those who refuse to worship the Beast will be taken to jail and executed/ or if they give in to the torture, they will receive the Mark Of The Beast, which is the RFID Chip; it will be placed in you right hand or your forehead.

- **<u>The Rapture</u> :**The Book Of Revelations chapter 7, verse 14, tells us that this momentous event will happen during the Great Tribulation. Those who believe in Jesus Christ and have lived Holy Lives will be taken away from the earth. **<u>Those</u>**

whom are left behind will have to endure the Wrath of God and the Antichrist while having to live under the New World Order system. Depopulation is the agenda, which is both Propagated by the leaders in authority, and written out **verbatimly** in the **Bible**.

- **Mark Of The Beast :**During The Great Tribulation while the Antichrist is in power, the people of the earth will have to live under the Antichrist system. The Global Economy will have collapsed entirely, which **IS HAPPENING** right now. You will not be able to function unless you have this Mark (**RFID Chip**) in your Right Hand or Forehead. **If you are caught without one you will be taken to jail or executed on the spot.** If you do have one, your Eternal Fate will be sealed in the Lake the Fire and you will **STILL** have to survive the Depopulation Agenda, in which your chances of surviving are by default, extremely small.

- **The Return Of Jesus :**This will be the greatest event in all of human history as the Lord and Savior of all humanity will return with His heavenly host of angels. All of the people of the world will be Judged by God and will have to give an account for how we have lived our lives here on Earth. Our hearts must be Purified before God. Everything you do and say is being recorded in the spiritual realm and you will answer for it.

<u>Chapter 2</u>

<u>Preparation Details</u>

The Physical Preparation is 2ndary and also a very critical component to being prepared. There are a number of factors to consider when thinking about survival in the End Times. These things include but are not limited to :

A.)<u>**Location**</u> : Where do you CURRENTLY Live? It will not be safe for you to dwell in the <u>**inner city areas, densely populated neighborhoods and apartment complexes**</u>. Those places will be ripe with robberies and bloody violence. This is extremely serious material that you are taking in right now and it is imperative that you take heed! Stay out of sight and out mind. Stay away from large crowds/groups of people.

- It will be very wise for you to move out to a <u>**far away**</u> place, such as out in the country, or into a mountainous area. But if you are not able to, then you must be that much more prepared for survival. <u>**Martial Law will be declared and many people will be Brutally beaten, arrested and taken to Jail**</u>. You could very well find yourself in a situation that forces you to have to immediately relocate to another location. Therefore, you need to have a "Prep Bag", which is what you will take with you when you leave that place.

B.)<u>**People :**</u> Who are the People that you are around/will be around? You need to at least know who are the main people that you most certainly want/need to be around. <u>**Do not**</u> surround yourself with people that could become "Liabilities". When I say Liabilities I am referring to those people that could very well get you/your family captured or killed by the enemy(s). Foolish/Ignorant people, in other words, are those that you need to be far away from during this time.

- You must also consider food supplies; for however many people that you intend on being around, that's how much more food and other supplies you are going to need. It will be much harder for you if you are pregnant, carrying around a new born child and/or other with other small children. This is the raw and honest truth dear people and you really need to be ready as much as you can possibly be.

C.) **Food :** This is obviously a very important section. We must have the proper nutrition to remain in a stable healthy condition. You need to start stocking up on food and water now. The time to acquire these things is not while the crisis is unfolding. When the economy collapses, the corner stores, food markets, and practically every other business will be looted and cleared out.

- It will not be very safe at all for you to interact with people during that time. Most people will be desperate to survive and will do anything to stay alive. The darkest parts of the human heart will be exposed during this time in history. People are going to cannibalize each other just to stay alive. You must understand the magnitude of this dear people. Billions of people starving to death, no food or clean water readily available, you better believe that they will get extremely desperate.

- Canned goods and easy to preserve foods are going to take you a long way during this time. You won't be in a position nor will it be exactly wise to try and have a nice 5 course meal. You should be able to order MREs from online, which is a "ready to eat" meal which the army uses. If you're having to live your life on the run (many will have to), then you will have to carry what you can at first, then begin scavenging for food.

- Water is clearly an important thing to have during this time, for **there is coming a time in which there will be no clean or running water**. So with this being the case, it would be wise for you to have gallons of water stored up and/or cases of water bottles. If you are caught in a situation in which you don't have any water at all in your possession then you are really going to have to get creative. One of the items listed below in the "Supplies" category is a Water Purifier. This device will allow you to drink water that would normally be undrinkable due to contamination.

D.) **Medical :** Everyone that is with you needs to have their own first aid kits. The basic healing, preventive, etc types of materials are what you need to have in stock. This includes A&D Ointment, Bandages, Alcohol, etc. You also need to have your basic Hygiene items with you, Toothbrush, toothpaste, soap, etc.

- I strongly encourage you all to learn basic survival skills. For you could very well find yourself in a situation in which it all hits the fan when you are completely off guard, and completely unprepared. Therefore you must be ready at all times, for any and everything.

- This is also when having the right person would really come into play. If someone on your team well versed in the medical field then you should be alright; but if not you will have to know something.

E.)**Supplies :** You don't need the entire toolbox with you during this time, but there are a few critical items that you will need to have in your possession. Remember : As I Said in the previous section, you could be anywhere when the "SHTF" so you need to have the right mindset so that you can be able to function properly. I will only name a few items here as there are a number of them that you should ultimately obtain.

1.) Solar Powered Generator(s)

2.) Water Purifier

3.) Matches

4.) First Aid Kit

5.) Knife and Rope

6.) Walkie Talkies

7.) Personal Life Saving Backpack (Rappelling Backpack)

These are just a few things that come to mind when I think of supplies. Also again I stress the importance of knowing **basic survival skills** as they **will help tremendously**. I'm sure that you can and will come up with more items to have. And again, the more people you are with during this time, means the more of these supplies that you will need to have, alongside all of the other things mentioned in the rest of the guide. Another thing to note are the robbers and gangs that will be out in full fledge during this time.

Be cognizant of your environment and the people that are in your immediate environment. You **must be** extremely vigilant as people will be very desperate to survive and will do anything to preserve what life/livelihood they still have. No one must know of what you possess, or how "prepared" you are, for you will most likely be the first person they come to when it hall hits the fan big time. Most people simply blow off this information as if its irrelevant and "not going to happen". But rest assured, it is **happening right now**.

The next two chapters are copied and pasted directly from another published book by the Author, entitled, "The End Of Time". These two Chapters were placed in this book so as to give people a more in depth look at the things that are to come to pass here shortly.

Chapter 3

The Great Tribulation

This period in History begins in Chapter 6 of Revelations. Each horse is a metaphorical depiction of what will transpire during this time. The first half of the Great Tribulation (3 and half years), will be the timeframe of these horsemen coming to pass. If you align what each of them represent, to what is happening in the world today, and what will be happening, you will indeed see that we are in perfect alignment with Biblical Prophecies; specifically The Horsemen, who began the Judgments from God in the beginning of Chapter 6. I will only expand on the six seals here, and leave the rest for another release.

Other parts of Revelations are mentioned elsewhere in this book. In verse 2 of that Chapter, One of the four beasts revealed to John "a white horse: and he that sat on him had a bow; and a crown was given unto him: and he went forth conquering, and to conquer.

***This horseman represents a religious and political power that will conquer the world during this time. Many nations will be subject to this agenda unfolding. The Religious power represents the nation of Islam that is rapidly gaining Dominion in the World, via other parties involved. Islam will eventually be the "heavy handed" dominating spiritual force during this time in which the Antichrist will use forcibly. The Political Power represents the "Elite" and their "pawns" whom preside in several, various regions of the earth, setting up and establishing "their" agenda.

4. And there went out another horse that was red: and power was given to him that sat thereon to take peace from the earth, and that they should kill one another: and there was given unto him a great sword.

***This horse represents World War III and the social meltdown that will be happening around the world during this period. Peace being taken from the earth can only imply that the people of the world will be turned against one another. As we see, and as few of us discern, Racism continues to thrive and it is being used by elite powers to divide the people up and to bring the world and specifically America into yet another civil war. "And that they should kill one another: and there was given unto him a great "sword.", this part of the scripture tells us exactly what the people will be doing.

I have a separate section just for WWIII due to the magnitude of it. But just know that outside of how catastrophic that event will be itself, the domestic violence that will transpire throughout our communities during this season will be very bad. Not only that, but the rate/timeframe in which these things are going to be happening is upon us and unfolding right before our eyes. Armed militias will/are forming at this moment in hopes to protect their lives and their loved ones; or to fulfill to some misguided sense of "Patriotism". It is a very unwise thing to do and these militias are laughably outmanned and outgunned without a question.

5. And when he had opened the third seal, I heard the third beast say, Come and see. And I beheld, and lo a black horse; and he that sat on him had a pair of balances in his hand.

6. And I heard a voice in the midst of the four beasts say, A measure of wheat for a penny, and three measures of barley for a penny; and see thou hurt not the oil and the wine.

***This seal represents economic hardship. America is the most indebted nation in the world and is only getting worse. People seem to believe that everything is alright or is going to get better, which is completely not the case at all. There is period known as "Hyperinflation", which is what is being described in these scriptures. "A measure of wheat for a penny, and three measures of barley for a penny;", gives an exact replica of what the prices of goods and services will be like during these times. People simply will not be able to afford to survive.

7. And when he had the fourth seal, I heard the voice of the fourth beast say, Come and see.

8. And I looked, and behold a pale horse: and his name that sat on him was Death, and Hell followed with him. And power was given unto them over the fourth part of the earth, to kill with the sword, and with hunger, and with death, and with the beasts of the earth.

The fourth seal describes a scene of absolute sorrow and desperation. This is the time in which around 2 billion people will be depopulated from the planet. The enforcement of the laws and regulations will be brutal as the people will be under heavy oppression from the civil authorities. The hunger pains will come from people not being able to afford to eat as the cost of living will have risen far out of most people's reach. The beasts of the earth is still a little blurry to me in terms of how that will actually pan out; but it would seem as though it can be taken literal.

Dreadful times will be upon the people of the world as most of them will be rounded up and taken off to modern day concentration camps (FEMA Camps). There are several hundred of these camps all over America so I can only imagine how many "similar" camps there are all over the world. Martial law will be in full effect as the police force is being heavily militarized and risen to the next level of capability. Society as we know it will fall completely apart and there will be anarchy in the streets. Disease will plague the people as another form of chastisement for disobedience. Although these "plagues" are usually laboratory experiments which have been injected into someone/something and spread throughout the general populace. The Plague itself is going to kill many millions of people.

9. And when he had opened the fifth seal, I saw under the altar the souls of them that were slain for the word of God, and for the testimony which they held:

10. And they cried with a loud voice, saying, How long, O Lord, holy and true, dost thou not Judge and avenge our blood on them that dwell on the earth?

11. And white robes were given unto every one of them; and it was said unto them, that they should rest yet for a little season, until their fellow servants also and their brethren, that should be killed as they were, should be fulfilled.

This seal describes the martyrdom of Christians during this time. Jesus told us specifically in Matthew 24 that we would be hated of all men for His Name's Sake. This implies that we will be full time/entirely under the Antichrist New World Order system. Christians have been Martyred since the beginning of Christianity, but this season of Persecution will be far worse than any of the others. As we are seeing now, Christians are at this moment in time being killed in horrific manners in various parts of the world for their Faith.

They are being killed by followers of Islam; terrorist groups who are devoted to carrying out the direct and specific orders from their god Allah. Islam is the Rod that the Antichrist will use to oppress and kill people that do not follow his agenda. This religious belief is being propagated to the masses and they have been for some time now gaining much support and political clout to further "their" agenda. Christians here in America for the most part have no idea what's coming as they are being fed a whole heap of ear tickling sermons that only serve to keep them comfortable in their cozy lifestyle.

But not only will there be people from the religion of Islam killing Christians; it will also be "normal" everyday citizens who have been brainwashed by the Antichrist into believing that Christians are terrorists. God will have given them over to reprobate minds therefore anyone who does not completely follow Jesus Christ will be subject to the devices/deceptions of the enemy, as they already are for the most part. Christians will be hunted down like wild animals during this time and treated will evil intent. Many Brethren in Christ will fall away and reject Jesus during this time as it will simply be too much for them to bare. We will live in the wilderness, caves, underground, etc during this time.

12. And I beheld when he had opened the sixth seal, and, lo, there was a great earthquake; and the sun became black as sackcloth of hair, and the moon became as blood;

13. And the stars of heaven fell unto the earth, even as a fig tree casteth her untimely figs, when she is shaken of a mighty wind.

14. And the heaven departed as a scroll when it is rolled together; and every mountain and island were moved out of their places.

Throughout the Bible, God tells us that a Blood Moon will be the notable sign of His return. There is also a separate section on the Blood Moons. The earthquake described here in scripture will perhaps be the biggest to ever strike the world. Testimonies from people who have been shown this earthquake from God describe it as one that will tear America in half, literally. This earthquake is described more in a separate section but the scriptures following it paints a picture of everyone being afraid, supposing that Jesus has returned in the midst of it.

The Great Tribulation will be the worse time period in human history. As Jesus Himself said in Matthew 24 : 21; "For then shall be great tribulation, such as was not since the beginning of the world to this time, no, nor ever shall be. Many people have "heard" about this or are "familiar" with it, but very few have the slightest clue as to just how serious it will be. This is the period in which The Book Of Revelations and The New World Order Agenda will really be accelerated and fully manifested. Alongside this, it's the period in which most of the human population will be exterminated with Extreme Prejudice.

This period will begin when the Antichrist breaks the 7 year peace treaty with Israel. For those who have the eyes to see, they will immediately know that this is the time to flee towards a faraway place. People have refused to Repent and give their lives to Jesus Christ therefore God will give them over to Reprobate minds and allow them to be deceived by the Enemy on all fronts. Even some of the professing Christians will fall prey to the deceptions that are to befall this world, thus free handedly giving their hearts and minds over to the Antichrist during this time and forfeiting their free gift of eternal life and choosing instead to perish in the lake of fire.

The Bible gives specific numerical accountability of just how many people will die during this time. Now, if we look at whom God is using, to fulfill His Perfect will, you will see, that "their" agenda is to reduce the population to 500 million people. Now, let's assume that there are 7.5 Billion people in the world when this specific time of Great Tribulation begins. The Book Of Revelations States in Chapter 9 : 15 ; "And the four angels were loosed, which were prepared for an hour, and a day, and a month, and a year, for to slay the third part of men.".......

That is one third of the entire global population, or 33.3% people, or 2.5 Billion people. Who are the four angels that carried this out? Hmmmm…. Right after this are the horsemen, who slay another 3rd of the human population, 2.5 Billion people; that's 5 Billion people perished. Who are the horsemen? Those are Soldiers, most likely United Nations Soldiers. And where do the other 2 Billion come from? These are mentioned in Revelations 6 : 8 ; "And I looked, and behold a pale horse: and his name that sat on him was Death, and Hell followed him. And power was given unto them over the fourth part of the earth, to kill with the sword, and with hunger, and with death, and with the beasts of the earth." That fourth part of the earth is 25% of the human population, or 1.87 Billion(exact) People. If you do the math, that's right around 7 Billion people, which leaves around 500 million people left. This falls just about perfectly in line with Satan's New World Order agenda – how so? Because God is USING the leaders of this "New World Order" To carry out HIS plan. But these wicked and evil men actually believe that they are doing ALL OF THIS EVIL in their own "human" Wisdom, following after Satan.

For those of you that STILL don't believe in this after ALL of this being presented here, Here are a few quotes from very powerful, evil men who have worked behind the scenes at some point in history, or currently today, that have PUBLICLY promoted or gloated about this "agenda" of "theirs":**"We are not going to achieve a New World Order without paying for it in blood as well as in words and money."**

- Arthur Schlesinger Jr., 'The CFR Journal
Foreign Affairs', August 1975.

"No one will enter the New World Order unless he or she will make a pledge to worship Lucifer.

No one will enter the New Age unless he will take a Luciferian Initiation."

David Spangler, Director of Planetary Initiative, United Nations

"We shall have world government whether or not you like it, by conquest or consent."

Statement by Council on Foreign Relations

(CFR) member James Warburg to The Senate Foreign Relations Committee on February 17th, 1950

These men are not even realizing that they are promoting God's Word to come to pass. There are numerous more quotes from various other individuals that validate this, so if you STILL are "skeptical" then I can only conclude that you simply do not want to believe. I pray that you awaken before it's too late and receive Salvation from the Lord Jesus Christ. He is the only way to escape the worse of these things, specifically that being eternal hellfire. Sadly, most, if not all of the men and women who say such things as mentioned above actually want to go to hell, foolishly believing that they will be rewarded when they get there, not grasping the fact that they too will burn in hell for all eternity alongside Lucifer and the rest of the fallen angels.

Chapter 4

The Antichrist

The Antichrist is described in detail in the Bible. If you look at the current Political Roster of people in the world today, and allow God to guide you into the truth, you will know who he is. In Daniel, Chapter 7, and Revelations, Chapter 13, God describes to us who the Antichrist and False Prophet are, which will lead and deceive the whole world away from God. It will be Lucifer, the leader of the Fallen Angels from God's Heavenly Kingdom, whom Inhabit the Heart and Mind and manipulate the human vessel here on Earth. The False Prophet, as the title itself implies, is a religious figure who will serve as "2nd in command" during the Antichrist's reign.

1. And I stood upon the sand of the sea, and saw a beast rise up out of the sea, having seven heads and ten horns, and upon his horns ten crowns, and upon his heads the name of blasphemy.

    ***The seven heads represent the 7 kings of the earth and the 10 crowns represent 10 kingdoms. The Antichrist will have dominion over all of these of the Earth during this time. Revelations 13 : 2 ;

    "And the beast which I saw was like unto a leopard, and his feet were as the feet of a bear, and his mouth as the mouth of a lion: and the dragon gave him his power, and his seat, and great authority."

    ***This is a description of the Antichrist. These animal features come right from the vision which was shown to Daniel, of the four beasts.

    "The dragon gave him his power, and his seat, and great authority", is telling us that it is Lucifer that will give the human on earth his official "Antichrist" title. Again, discernment of the Holy Spirit will guide you into all truths.

2. And I saw one of his heads as it were wounded to death; and his deadly wound was healed: and all the world wondered after the beast.

***This scripture describes to us the actual scene, that will come to pass here on earth, which will alert us to when the Antichrist's time has officially began. His deadly wound can only come from 1 of 3 sources; accident, assassination attempt, false flag attack. Either way, shortly thereafter his wound will be healed; either by laying on of hands from some high ranking religious figure, or just another part to a grander deception against the masses. And of course, an event of this magnitude with this type of outcome would have a huge impact on those who are not awake.

3. And they worshipped the dragon which gave power to the beast: and they worshipped the beast, saying, Who is like unto the beast? Who is able to make war with him?

   ***Here we are being told that the people will so given to the satanic system, after being taken astray by the deadly wound, that they are going to worship the devil himself, and the Antichrist. They will defend him, reverence him, follow his every order (or be executed).

4. And there was given unto him a mouth speaking great things and blasphemies; and power was given unto him to continue forty and two months.

   ***The Antichrist will be very foul mouthed against God and the Body Of Christ. He will "Blasphemy" God and speak extensively proud in his attitude. He will also be given power "TO CONTINUE" forty and two months. "To Continue" tells us that he had already been in power – he was given an "extended" period of time to have his authority. Forty and two months is 3 and a half years, which is the 2nd half of the Great Tribulation period. Revelations 13 :

6. "And he opened his mouth in blasphemy against God, to blaspheme his name, and his tabernacle, and them that dwell in heaven.

7. And it was given unto him to make war with the saints, and to overcome them: and power was given him over all kindreds, and tongues, and nations.

8. And all that dwell upon the earth shall worship him, whose names are not written in the book of Life of the Lamb slain from the foundation of the world.

9. If any man have an ear, let him hear.

10. He that leadeth into captivity shall go into captivity: he that killeth with the sword
must be killed with the sword. Here is the patience and the faith of the saints."

*** These scriptures tell us that not only will the Antichrist blaspheme the Body Of
Christ, but he will war against it/Christians. We are also told that he will overcome us
and have dominion over the entire world. Everyone who's name isn't written in
the Book Of Life will worship him. It is during this period that the people who reject
him, will live their lives on the run, which is described in verse 10. The saints of God will
truly be tested like never before during this time.

Everyone who does not worship the image of the beast/Antichrist will be put to death, as spoken
in Revelations 13 : 15;

"And he had power to give life unto the image of the beast, that the image of the
beast should both speak, and cause that as many as would not worship the image of
the beast should be killed." Billions of people will perish during this season of
Global Persecution, especially the Christians. The image of the Beast
will be created via a long term construct in the making named "Project Blue Beam", as
mentioned in Revelations 13 : 14;

"And deceiveth them that dwell on the earth BY THE MEANS of those miracles which
 he had power to do in the sight of the beast; saying to them that dwell on the earth, that
they should make an image to the beast, which had the wound by a sword, and did live."

"By the means" that is spoken of in he scripture above is telling us there is a specific
method/ process/ technology that will allow the 2nd Beast to carry out these deceptions. I will not
go into detail here as to what Project Blue Beam is so I encourage you all to do your due
diligence so that you can get a very clear understanding as to what it is and what role it has
played and will play in the coming time(s). Most people will be as they are today, completely
deceived and living in a world of absolute disillusionment. As sad as this is, this is simply the
world that we live in. People would much rather sit around and watch TV all day than make the
necessary changes to their lives that would solidify their position in the Kingdom Of Heaven.

Who is the Antichrist? I will not state his name here, but I strongly urge you all to ask
the Lord to lead you to the answer. But I will tell you that he is in fact in power right now. All of
you have most certainly seen or heard of him before. God will indeed allow this man to
persecute the entire world and trample it under foot at his will.

Most people will die horrible deaths and be forced to undergo brutal suffering and punishment. Honestly, words will never be able to describe the level at which this is going to occur; search your hearts right now dear people; allow the Lord God, Jesus Christ into your lives so that you may be counted worthy to inherit His Eternal Kingdom.

All of you whose names are not written in God's Book of Life will bow down and be forced to accept the Mark Of The Beast. You will worship and reverence him day and night or be executed or tortured beyond what you could ever possibly imagine. Or you will have to live your life in captivity for the rest of your days until it's all over with. From this point many people will starve to death or resort to cannibalizing each other for survival, since they will not be able to buy or sell anything unless they have his Mark. And when I say captivity, I mean that you will be living in mountains, caves, forests, wooded locations, underground, etc.

You simply will have no other choice of survival. If you remain in the cities and try to survive, it will only be a matter of time before you are captured or killed by the "Police/military" forces. The police will be Judge, Jury, and Executioner on the spot. It will be at their sole discretion as to rather or not you will live if they capture you without the Mark Of The Beast. But in most cases, they will in fact choose to execute you.

You think police brutality is bad now? Just wait until all of THIS begins to come to pass. Dear readers, I implore you to Understand the Magnitude of these Circumstances, and to also Know and internalize the Fact that it is not my Father's Will that you Perish, without first Knowing His Son Jesus Christ as your Lord And Savior.

For the Brethren In Christ whom are Left Behind; you must be strong in the Faith. If you are captured by the Enemy, it is critical that you are able to endure whatever pain and suffering the Antichrist puts you through. That very short period of time of suffering will be nothing compared to the Eternal Glory that you are to inherit in God's Eternal Kingdom. That is assuming you have purified your hearts and are no longer operating in Iniquity. Many of the Brethren In Christ Will Renounce Jesus under the immense pressure and will snap like a twig as if they never knew Jesus during this time.

Many of my fellow Brethren are very "gung ho" about being Martyred for Jesus. Although this is a very valiant and honorable thing, perhaps one of the highest honors, it is critical that you are HUMBLE and that you PRAY for the STRENGTH to endure. Being Martyred is not some cake walk dear Brethren. Yes, there are already 10s of thousands of

Guillotines awaiting us who believe; but take serious note Brethren; if you are chosen to be Beheaded, you are seriously blessed. To elaborate on this I mean that you could have easily been chosen to undergo days of horrifying torture instead, which would yield an exponentially higher chance of you rejecting Jesus and accepting the Mark Of The Beast.

And Of Course, God tells us in Revelations that all of those who accept The Mark Of The Beast will burn and spend an Eternity separated from God in The Lake of Fire. God does not want this for you dear people but it is the inevitable and only outcome for all of those who reject His Free Gift of Salvation through His Only Begotten Son Jesus Christ. Your money, fame, power, authority, popularity, intellect, etc, are completely irrelevant and will not matter one inch when it is all said and done. God is not a respecter of persons therefore everyone will be on equal standing and Judged righteously according to His Holy Word. There is no other way around this dear people so I truly hope that you decide right now at this moment where you want to spend eternity.

<u>A Final Word</u>

I truly Desire to see you all in my Father's Kingdom. We are right here in the midst of a fiery storm that is engulfing the entire world. You have to know that YOU are Eternally secure, then those around you. I know that you, and myself included, want to see our loved ones in heaven when we leave this earth. We must plant that seed into their hearts and minds, and it is God that brings the Harvest.

You must Understand that these are serious times upon us and you and your loved ones will be tested beyond what you can imagine. That is why I hope and pray with all my heart and mind that you are taking heed to what I have spoken to you in this guide. Do not be fearful of these things that are to come to pass. Simply trust in Jesus like never before, and Embrace these times, for Eternity is literally upon us. We have but a short time left to be here on this planet.

Be Faithful to God and teach your loved ones to do the same. Do not go out at night times unless you really need to. Please use basic Wisdom; Aseasy as that may sound, most people will simply not possess it during this time. Everyone will be acting out of full throttle emotional desperation. You and your loved ones will have to stick together and trust in each other at an all new level.

It is my earnest desire that you accept the FREE gift of Salvation of Today. It does not cost you anything. God desires to have you in His Kingdom, and it is only through His Only Begotten Son Jesus Christ that we can Inherit It. There are no other ways to Heaven and that is being shown in so many ways in these times that are upon us now. Do not be Deceived by the lies that are out here in the World today, for the deception is only going to get much worse from.

This is why its so Imperative that you be filled with the Truth of God inside of you. That way you are able to Discern the evil that is upon this land. Again I say, "Most" People are not in tune with these things so YOU need to be one of the few that are ready when it all hits the fan. Contact me so that we can talk about these things in more detail.